P9-DOD-448

THE UPPER ROOM CHAPEL

THE LAST SUPPER

The Story of the Leonardo da Vinci Masterpiece

by

HOWARD W. ELLIS

The Upper Room

The World's Most Widely Used Devotional Guide

and

Other Devotional Literature

1908 Grand Avenue

Nashville, Tennessee 37203

Library of Congress Catalog Card
Number: 63-19190

The Scripture quotations in this book, unless otherwise indicated, are from the Revised Standard Version of the Bible, copyrighted 1946 and 1952 by the Division of Christian Education of the National Council of Churches, and are used by permission.

UR—183-15-0963
Printed in the United States of America

To

my wife

SUSANNA

whose unfailing affection
and incomparable devotion
constantly demonstrate the
deep meaning of Christian
communion

CONTENTS

ILLUSTRATIONS

FOREWORD

We are glad to present this volume on *The Last Supper* by Howard W. Ellis. Here at the home of *The Upper Room* in Nashville, Tennessee, we have what is said to be the largest wood carving of Leonardo da Vinci's *Last Supper*. It was done by Ernest Pellegrini and is life size. It has become world renowned. Many visitors come daily to see The Upper Room Chapel and *The Last Supper*. Many ask about a book which tells something of the masterpiece. This book has come into being because of these requests. Howard Ellis has been a student of Leonardo's masterpiece for years. He is an artist in his own right and a well-known religious youth worker. He has often reproduced the Last Supper in his paintings. One of these reproductions is on pages 56 and 57 of this book.

The author has given some background on the observance of the Passover, which was the occasion for the Last Supper. He discusses the work of Leonardo and his original painting in Milan, Italy.

There is a character study of each of the disciples and then, of course, the discussion of what has been called "the saddest face in all history."

We take pleasure in presenting this book as an interpretation of the Last Supper with special reference to the wood carving in The Upper Room Chapel. Mr. Ellis has lived with the picture and knows it. He handles it sympathetically and reverently. It is hoped that the book may be a blessing to many.

—J. Manning Potts
Editor, *The Upper Room*
Nashville, Tennessee

I

THE PASSOVER FESTIVAL

Jesus, the author and finisher of our faith, was a Jew. On the last night before His crucifixion He met His disciples in the upper room for their final Passover meal.

What is the Passover? How did it originate? What is this festival that brought Jesus to Jerusalem?

There is much uncertainty about the history of the Passover, but by putting together the various facts available we get some idea of how it came to be. *The Union Haggadah,* a book by the Central Conference of American Rabbis, traces the Passover to its origin in the misty dawn of history. We must go back across the long centuries to the days of pre-Israelite history, for this Passover feast has its roots in one of the oldest and most sacred sacraments known to mankind. It was the custom among nomadic peoples, wandering herdsmen, to offer up the firstborn of their flocks to the deity in order to be blessed with an increase in the flocks for the coming year. We see the ancient altars with their sacrifices on almost every page of certain sections of the Old Testament. To the people of those early days blood had life-giving qualities. Men celebrated the blood covenant because it bound them to their God and to one another as nothing else could. When you see in the Old Testament the smoke from these altar fires, remember man is celebrating the blood covenant.

The Israelites were wandering herdsmen before they became tillers of the soil; therefore the sacrificing of the lamb is the oldest part of the Passover service. When the wandering Israelite shepherds settled in Canaan, their new neighbors

were an agricultural people. Their farm neighbors celebrated
the new harvest with the baking of bread and the offering
of the firstfruit of the good earth in gratitude for harvest-
time. Gradually the two festivals became one—the festivals
of the harvest and the slaughtering of the lamb.

When the people of Israel followed Joseph into Egypt,
they took with them their spring festivities. They went into
Egypt as friends. But later the Pharaohs took over as masters,
and the people of Israel became their slaves.

Then Moses becomes the children of Israel's leader. He
intercedes on behalf of his people before Pharaoh. Recorded
in Exodus 5:3 is one of Moses' pleas to Pharaoh which gives
evidence in favor of the suggestion that the children of
Israel were already observing a festival similar to the Passover
before they went into Egypt. Moses begs Pharaoh: "Let us go,
we pray thee, three days' journey into the desert and sacrifice
unto the Lord our God." Bible scholars believe that the sacrifice Moses referred to is similar to that of the Passover.

The Bible tells us of the marvelous leadership Moses gives
on behalf of freeing his people from Egyptian bondage. He
tries in every way to persuade Pharaoh to let his people go.
One plague after another strikes the Egyptians. Finally the
angel of death takes even the king's son, and the Pharaoh
gives the order that sets the people free.

The people of Israel are probably beginning their spring
celebration when the order comes to move out. Hastily they
kill their lambs, smear blood on their door lintels, eat a hasty
meal, and begin to move out of slavery to the land of freedom
their Lord has promised them beyond the horizon across the
Red Sea to the north.

Ever afterward the Passover has been their festival of freedom. Through the years the observance of this festival has
varied. During the time Jesus lived on earth, the week's cele-

bration began in the Temple at sunset on Friday—the beginning of the Hebrews' Sabbath. Each family took a lamb to the Temple where it was killed and then dedicated by the priests. Then the lamb was taken home and roasted whole. The small family invited in its closest relatives and friends. Then at night each family ate its lamb with the unleavened bread, *matzoth,* and bitter herbs. The celebration continued for a week. This memorial feast is often called the Feast of Unleavened Bread because the eating of the unleavened bread is an important part of the feast.

It was this festival, the Passover, that brought Jesus to Jerusalem the last week of His life and to the upper room on the last night of His life.

This ancient festival is observed in Jewish homes today with little change from the way it was observed in the days of Jesus. We have already described how in those days the lamb was prepared for the meal. This festival meal presents a historical drama—a drama of deliverance of a people from Egyptian slavery.

The cup of each guest plays an important part in the ritual. During the meal each person's cup is filled four times. A benediction is said over the first cup of wine. With the second cup, the firstborn son asks his father four questions about the meaning of the meal. The drama unfolds as the questions are answered. Then Psalms 113 and 114 are sung. The main course of the meal is then eaten and the third cup drunk. With the fourth cup comes the singing of Psalms 115-118.

The four cups of wine taken during the festival meal are in remembrance of the covenant God made to His people when He led them out of bondage into the promised land (Exodus 6:6-8). At His farewell meal with His disciples, Jesus took the cup and made it the symbol of His covenant with His disciples. Phillips' translation of Luke 22:20 reads,

"He gave them a cup after supper with the words: 'This cup is the new agreement made in my own blood which is shed for you.' "

Thus Jesus takes the occasion and the symbolism of this sacred rite of His people—the Passover—and uses the sacred bread and cup to impress upon His disciples what He is about to do for them and for all mankind—die upon a cross that they may live.

THE LAST SUPPER
The Painting by Leonardo da Vinci

"When it was evening, he sat at table with the twelve disciples; and as they were eating, he said, 'Truly, I say to you, one of you will betray me.'" In Matthew 26:17-30 we are told about the Last Supper that Jesus kept with His disciples. It is this event that Leonardo da Vinci has depicted in his painting *The Last Supper*.

LEONARDO DA VINCI

The story of the life and work of Leonardo da Vinci reads like a fairy tale. From childhood he attracted attention for his unusual ability to learn. He was handsome in appearance and popular with the courtiers of Italy. He was an athlete with muscles so powerful that he could bend iron bars with his bare hands. Yet he was so kindly that he sometimes purchased cages of birds just to set them free.

He began his art career by studying under Andrea del Verrocchio. From the first the brilliant and gifted Leonardo displayed rare talent. He soon surpassed his master teacher.

Leonardo da Vinci is doubtless one of the most versatile geniuses who ever lived. Painting was only one of the many fields he mastered.

Leonardo holds a unique place in the Italian Renaissance and the history of art. Up to the latter part of the fifteenth century nothing much had been done in the world of art since ancient times. Then suddenly Italy produced a number of contemporary artists who rank among the world's all-time greatest: Raphael, Michelangelo, Titian, Corregio, and Leonardo da Vinci.

Leonardo and Michelangelo are the giants of the Renaissance. But Leonardo stands alone in the universal nature of his genius, in the intellectual sensitivity of his art, and in the influence of his life and work. More than any other man, he was the architect and guiding genius of the Italian Renaissance.

His father was a notary at Florence and a middle-class citizen of Vinci. Leonardo was a child prodigy. He grew up at Vinci and went to Florence in his youth when his father moved there.

Though Leonardo received only the ordinary training of a poor boy in Florence, he made good use of his capacity for self-education. His mind encompassed a wide range of knowledge. He was a sculptor; he was a musician; he was a painter; he was a poet; and he was an architect. He worked for a time as an architect on the cathedral of Milan.

He was a chemist; he was a machinist; he was an engineer; and he was an inventor. He developed working designs for both a steamship and an airplane.

He studied botany and probed into the science of anatomy. He drew some of the first medical art pictures ever produced. He was well on the way to learning about the circulation of the blood and made sketches of his discovery.

He was a geologist and an astronomer. He understood the motion of the earth and the effect of the moon upon the tides. He was familiar with the meaning of fossil shells and estimated the age of the earth.

He experimented with water pressure and developed the science of hydraulics. He invented a workable hydrometer and brought out a worm gear that was the forerunner of the gear in the modern automobile.

If engineers had been able to build his models of steamboats and airplanes he was able to design on his drawing board, we might have been in the air age soon after Columbus discovered America! Certainly Leonardo would be at home in the twentieth century!

Unfortunately, his handwriting is so bad that deciphering it is almost impossible. He wrote with his left hand, backhanded, and from right to left. It is only recently that translators have deciphered and published all that he wrote.

We have been almost five hundred years catching up with many of his theories and ideas. Yet his biographers lament the fact that he spent so much time in court functions and social affairs that he never fully applied his tremendous powers.

After his childhood years at Vinci, Leonardo spent many years in Florence and also in Milan. He went to Rome in 1513 and from there to France in 1516 or 1517. He died in France in May, 1519. He will always be remembered for his two paintings: the world's greatest portrait *Mona Lisa* and the world's greatest religious masterpiece *The Last Supper*.

HISTORY OF *THE LAST SUPPER*

Authorities are not certain as to the exact date Leonardo began work on *The Last Supper*. He probably started it in 1495, and there is evidence that he had it almost finished in 1497. The painting was a memorial to Beatrice, the wife of the Duke of Milan. Leonardo designed the picture as a mural painting for the refectory, or dining hall, of a building connected with the Church of St. Mary of the Graces in Milan.

Leonardo experimented with this picture. Before his time, murals were done in fresco. This meant that the artist had to plaster and paint at the same time, letting his paint dry in the plaster. Leonardo saw the limitations of this hurried method. He began to experiment with oils over the plaster.

Unfortunately, his surface was entirely unsuited for an oil painting. The picture began to flake and peel within ten years. Fifty years later it was nearly ruined. Cracks began to appear; damp and dust covered the surface; great chunks of the plaster fell away.

As though that were not enough, the careless custodians of the building cut a door in the wall in remodeling the hall in the seventeenth century. They cut off the Savior's feet in the picture.

In 1796 Napoleon stabled his cavalry horses in the hall. It is said that the soldiers amused themselves by throwing stones at the figures of the Master and His twelve disciples. The hall was used as a stable and a hayloft.

The worst desecration of the picture came years later under the Austrians. They nailed the coat of arms of Austria to the wall over the head of Christ!

So many restorers have worked on the picture that it is hard to tell what is left of the original. The beauty of the painting can be seen through some of the contemporary re-creations. One of the most famous reproductions is the stained glass window in the Court of Honor in Forest Lawn Memorial Park, Glendale, California. Ernest Pellegrini, America's best-known sculptor in wood, did what is perhaps the finest polychrome wood carving of *The Last Supper*. It is the center of worship in The Upper Room Chapel, Nashville, Tennessee.

THE TECHNIQUE OF THE PICTURE

Leonardo devoted his best thought and skill to this picture at the prime of his life. The picture required a great amount of time. He took each character from life. His notebooks reveal his search for the characterizations and the design and arrangement that would best portray this scene.

One of his great problems was to avoid monotony. He chose to group his figures on one side of a long table, open to view. He took the tables used in the dining hall as the prototype for the table in the painting. Thus Christ sits at the table as the constant guest of those who break bread together in the refectory. The tablecloth with its knotted corners is like the linen used in this room in Leonardo's day.

Leonardo made no attempt to re-create the physical setting of the upper room of Jesus' day. Had he done so, he would have been compelled to picture the disciples on low couches around a table, eating in a reclining position.

He endeavored to capture the moment when Jesus said: "One of you will betray me."

The windows behind Christ open on a typical Italian landscape. The open windows relieve the pent-up atmosphere of this moment.

Critics have said that if you would mask the faces the dramatic pantomime of the hands alone would tell the story. The hands help to pull the picture together.

The artist placed Christ in the center of the picture. The lines of perspective converge on the Savior—the lines of the floor, of the ceiling, of the walls all meet at the face of Christ. The tangle of arms, the gestures of the disciples—all lead us back to the Master. Leonardo divides his long expanse of table into five equally divided portions. He uses the horizontal line as his basic format for the picture. A group of three forms a psychological unit. Christ occupies the center section. The more prominent of the disciples are near Him, and the less prominent ones are at the ends of the table.

Technically, this picture is one of the most perfect in the world. We know from Leonardo's notebooks that he sketched and experimented, arranged and rearranged, and finally hit upon this design by trial and error. We cannot imagine a better arrangement.

Years of study went into producing this painting. Many beautiful legends have gathered about the picture. It is a matter of history that Leonardo made his sketches in his studio with meticulous care. Then he traced them on the walls. Consequently he would be away from his work in the refectory for days at a time. Then he would rush frantically in from the hot streets of the city, mount the scaffolding, and paint furiously for a few hours. Then he would disappear again—for days.

The prior of the place became quite frustrated by Leonardo's performance. He wanted the picture finished so that he could get the artist's scaffolding down. He thought that Leonardo should get on with his painting, and he told Leonardo as much. He was constantly urging him to hurry. And no wonder!

Leonardo sometimes stood for hours at a time, studying his work intently, not moving out of his tracks. The prior with his prodding got on Leonardo's nerves. Confiding to a friend that he was having trouble finding someone to pose for Judas, Leonardo said, "If I continue to search in vain I shall have to use the prior's head. It would serve well for the purpose."

Leonardo was a kindly man, and someone gives us these words as his reply to the prior: "A picture is not wrought by hands alone, good father, but by thought, In the inner life it must first start and grow to form and color in the soul."

Let us turn now to a study of the personalities revealed by this picture of the passion.

III

A CHARACTER STUDY OF THE DISCIPLES

The disciples spent one day of Holy Week preparing for the Passover. This is the most sacred of all Jewish festivals. One reason Jesus and His disciples came to the Holy City was to celebrate this religious festival. They prepared for it in the upper room. Friends in Jerusalem gave them a meeting place in their home. Tradition names the mother of John Mark as their hostess. Jesus told His disciples that He had anticipated this supper with great desire. And on the last night of His life He sat down to eat with His chosen companions and presided at the Passover meal.

The artist pictures Jesus at the table with the twelve. "And as they were at the table eating, Jesus said, 'Truly, I say to you, one of you will betray me, one who is eating with me' " (Mark 14:18). This is the moment that the artist pictures. The disciples are shocked by Jesus' announcement. Their hearts are heavy. They say one after another, "Is it I?"

Jesus says, "It is one of the twelve, one who is dipping bread in the same dish with me."

Now He takes the bread and blesses it and breaks it, giving it to them and saying, "This is my body which is broken for you. Do this in remembrance of me" (I Cor. 11:24).

Then Jesus takes a cup and gives thanks, perhaps offering the ancient prayer of gratitude found in the Passover ritual in *The Union Haggadah*: "Praised art Thou, O Lord our God, Ruler of the world, who hast created the fruit of the vine."

As He gives it to them, He says:

"Drink of it, all of you; for this is my blood of the covenant, which is poured out for many for the forgiveness of sins. I tell you I shall not drink again of this fruit of the vine until that day when I drink it new with you in my Father's kingdom" (Matt. 26:28-29).

Leonardo's genius and insight are nowhere better demonstrated than in the character study he makes of each of the disciples. He captures with his brush that dramatic moment when the Master announces: "One of you will betray me."

Every man reacts in his own way to the crisis of this particular moment. Each portrait is a study in temperament.

JOHN, JUDAS, AND PETER

Let us study first the group of disciples which has John, Judas, and Peter in it. To the right of the Master, in the place of honor, is John. Leaning over to speak to him is Peter. And between them, clutching the moneybag, is Judas.

JOHN

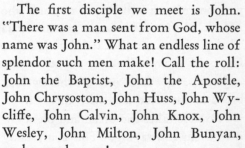

John*

The first disciple we meet is John. "There was a man sent from God, whose name was John." What an endless line of splendor such men make! Call the roll: John the Baptist, John the Apostle, John Chrysostom, John Huss, John Wycliffe, John Calvin, John Knox, John Wesley, John Milton, John Bunyan, John R. Mott. What an honored name!

Scholars believe that there are two or three men named John who had a hand in making New Testament history. It could be said of each of these men that there was a man "sent from God, whose name was John."

---

* In the Pentecost Window in The Upper Room Chapel is a set of symbols for the apostles. This symbol of John and those of the other apostles carried in this chapter are from the Pentecost Window.

PETER, JUDAS, JOHN

We can see two different men before us here. First, there is the John of legend and art, the beloved Disciple. Artists portray him as a mystic, as very modest—the unnamed disciple identified in the Fourth Gospel as the one who leans upon Jesus' breast at the Last Supper.

This is the man Leonardo portrays: His face is kind and tender. He sits at the right hand of Jesus—at the place of honor. He is the only one at the table who feels himself above reproach. He is not protesting, "Lord, is it I?" He sits in broken-hearted silence. This is the John of tradition and art. He is quiet and unassuming. He wears no beard. He has a winsome face and an eager, youthful spirit, unburdened by the worries and cares of maturity.

But the John we meet in the Synoptic Gospels is the son of Zebedee—a different type of person altogether. He is one of the brothers Jesus calls the "sons of thunder."

Look at the record. John and his brother James are seen at the center of strife that arises among the disciples. James and John come boldly to Jesus on the journey to Jerusalem and say: "Teacher, we want you to do for us whatever we ask of you."

Jesus asks them, "What do you want me to do for you?"

They answer, "Grant us to sit, one at your right hand and one at your left, in your glory."

But Jesus quizzes them, "You do not know what you are asking. Are you able to drink the cup that I drink, or to be baptized with the baptism with which I am baptized?"

They assure Him, "We are able."

Jesus then informs them, "The cup that I drink you will drink; and with the baptism with which I am baptized, you will be baptized; but to sit at my right hand or at my left is not mine to grant, but it is for those for whom it has been prepared."

The other disciples were indignant at James and John. But Jesus called them together and gave them His principle for true greatness. He said: "Whoever would be great among you must be your servant, and whoever would be first among you must be slave of all. For the Son of man also came not to be served but to serve, and to give his life a ransom for many."

Leonardo has placed James and John, these brothers who are in the inner circle, at the right and left hand of Jesus. But apparently they still needed to learn the lessons Jesus had been teaching them in Galilee.

This is the John we meet in the gospel story: He is a man of temper, hotheaded, ambitious. Yet his fellowship with the Master is unbroken. We find him at the right hand of the Master, and His obedient servant on the night of the Last Supper.

There is the legend that John lived in Ephesus during the closing years of his life. When he addressed the congregation, always he pronounced this benediction: "Beloved, let us love one another." This is the John Leonardo portrays.

"Beloved, we are God's children now; it does not yet appear what we shall be, but we know that when he appears we shall be like him, for we shall see him as he is."

Matthias*

JUDAS

Here is the man whose name is— traitor! In the drama of Holy Week, he plays the role of the villain. For nineteen centuries he has borne the cursed name of traitor to the Son of Man. His name is—Judas.

Leonardo leaves us with no doubt as to the identity of the betrayer at the supper table. His dark, cunning face; his

* The Upper Room Pentecost Window carries the symbol of the man who was chosen to take the place of Judas.

deep-set eyes; his swift movement as he instinctively recoils from the others—all betray the betrayer. The features of Judas betray fear and anger, excitement and resentment.

Yet he is one of the twelve invited to the upper room to break bread at the Last Supper with the Master of men.

He clutches in his hand the moneybag, symbol of his undoing. In his agitation, Judas upsets the saltcellar with his elbow. The spilling of salt is an ominous sign of ill fortune.

Less renowned artists have isolated Judas from the others—alone at the end of the table or in the act of leaving the table. But Leonardo isolates him psychologically rather than physically. His striking characterization of Judas is a masterful touch on the part of the artist.

The long-awaited hour is at hand. The guest room has been furnished with meticulous care. The meal has been prepared. The Passover wine and bread are ready. At last the apostles are alone in the upper room with their Lord.

We can hear Jesus as He says: "I have earnestly desired to eat this passover with you before I suffer; for I tell you I shall not eat it until it is fulfilled in the kingdom of God."

No one quite understands at first what He is saying; but while they are eating, He makes it plain. He says: "Truly, I say to you, one of you will betray me." This is the moment Leonardo da Vinci has captured—forever.

Instantly these men are cut to the bottom of their hearts. We hear them raise their voices in disbelief.

These words come like a thunderbolt to Judas. He has been found out! He recoils from his Master, smitten by his guilty conscience. Yet he, too, echoes the exclamations of the other disciples who say: "Is it I?"

Peter cannot wait for Jesus to identify the betrayer. He pushes his way past Judas to John and says, "Tell us who it is of whom he speaks."

John, who is at Jesus' side, says to Him, "Lord, who is it?" The disciples keep looking at one another, talking among themselves. Anxiously now they wait for Jesus to explain.

Jesus says: "The man who has just dipped his hand with me in the dish is the man who is going to betray me. The Son of Man is going away as the Scriptures say of Him, but a curse will be on that man by whom He is betrayed. It would have been better for that man, if he had never been born!" (Matt. 26:23-24. Williams) *

Then Judas, who even now has betrayed Him, asks: "Is it I, Master?"

Jesus says, "You have said so."

Judas knows now he cannot bear to stay in this upper room another minute. As soon as Jesus gives him his piece of bread, he rises and leaves the room quickly and goes out into the night with the words of Jesus ringing in his ears: "What you are going to do, do quickly."

We have questions about this apostle. Who can know Judas' thoughts as he leaves his place in the upper room? Why did he want to share in this sacrament of bread and wine? What prompts him to break the sacred covenant of the Passover meal? What motives drive him to betray his Master with a kiss?

No one suspects Judas. No one is pointing his finger at him. The others think he is about his business even yet, buying food for the group, perhaps, or giving something to the poor.

Each one is wondering in his heart if he has inadvertently betrayed his Lord. "Is it I, Lord?"

But Judas goes out and plays the villain. And it is night— a night of infamy. He goes out to confirm to his enemies that

---

* Charles B. Williams, *The New Testament: A Translation in the Language of the People,* Bruce Humphries, publisher, 1937. Used by permission of Moody Press, Chicago, Ill.

there is no doubt about it: Jesus is the man they are seeking.

There are a thousand excuses we might offer for Judas. The fact remains that while the eleven others are gradually surrendering their lives to their Lord's will and purpose, Judas is withholding his own. While the miracle of character transformation is working in them, Judas remains unchanged. He chooses to play the role of the informer in history's darkest tragedy.

PETER

Peter

Directly behind Judas is Peter. He is leaning over, trying to get John's attention. This is Peter the big, rough fisherman, with blunt manners and a runaway tongue. Hotheaded one moment and apologetic the next, he is above all a man of action. In any list of the disciples, his name is always first: "Simon, who is called Peter" and then the others.

Perhaps the reason for his prominence among the apostles is that he is always saying something, always doing something, always taking the lead.

See him as he springs to action in this upper room scene. He watches in amazement as the Master gets up from the table, takes off His outer garments, and fastens a towel about His waist. What is the Master doing? He pours water into the basin, takes a towel, and begins to wash the disciples' feet. Why, this is the work of a servant! And now He comes to Simon Peter. The following account is according to the Williams translation:

"Lord, are you going to wash my feet?"

"You do not now understand what I am doing, but by and by you will learn."

Peter says, "You must never wash my feet!"

Jesus replies, "Unless I do wash you, you can have no share with me."

"Lord, do not stop with my feet then, but wash my hands and face too!"

This is just like Peter. It is all or nothing with him.

After washing Peter's feet, Jesus takes His garments and resumes His place. Jesus says, "Do you understand what I have done to you? You call me Teacher and Lord, and you are right in calling me so, for that is what I am. If I then, your Lord and Teacher, have washed your feet, you too ought to wash one another's feet."

In the midst of their discussion about His going away, Jesus tells them, "I am going where you cannot follow me just now, but you will later follow me."

Peter speaks up, "Lord, why can I not follow you right now? I will lay down my life for you."

Jesus answers, "You will lay down your life for me! I most solemnly say to you, before a cock crows, you will three times disown me!"

Notice that in Leonardo's representation Peter in his excitement has the hilt of his bread knife almost against Judas' back. This portrait of Peter is true to life.

We may well wonder why Jesus chose Peter to be one of the twelve, a man who can so quickly promise one thing and immediately do the opposite. And yet on this night of their Last Supper together Jesus looks beyond Simon bar-Jona to the new Peter, the rock. The Master sees in Peter's faith the rock on which He can build His Church and the gates of hell cannot prevail against it. He sees the strength around which all the other disciples will rally to begin proclaiming the Kingdom of God, the mission entrusted to them on this night of the Last Supper.

What was it that Peter remembered after His tragic betrayal when he came face to face with Jesus?

I believe he remembered this great moment at the table during the Last Supper when Jesus said "Simon, Simon, listen! Satan has asked permission to sift all of you like wheat, but I have prayed especially for you that your own faith may not utterly fail. And you yourself, after you have turned, must strengthen your brothers" (Luke 22:31-32. Williams).

JAMES THE GREATER, THOMAS, AND PHILIP

These first three disciples at the right of the Master are a study in contrasts. Now our eyes are drawn to the group at the Master's left hand in this festival of the Kingdom. In the second group of disciples are James, in front; Thomas, standing just behind him; and Philip, farther over.

James the Greater

JAMES THE GREATER

As we read the Gospels, we see that three of the disciples are closer to the Master than the others—"Peter and James and John." How often we hear these three named!

James is the silent member of this triumvirate around Jesus. These chosen three seem always to be in the center of the Master's attention. They are the inner circle.

They are there when the Master lays His hands on the daughter of Jairus. And they see Jesus dismiss the mourners as He says: "Go away, for the girl is not dead, but is sleeping" (Matt. 9:24. Williams). Some laughed in the Master's face, but not these three. They are at His side when He takes the girl by the hand and brings her back to life and health, restoring her to the fellowship of her family.

They are there with their Lord on the Mount of Transfiguration. These three stand with their Lord in this hour of matchless beauty. They look into His face; they feel the presence of Moses and Elijah; they see who Jesus is. They hear a voice from the eternal saying, "This is my beloved Son . . . ; listen to him."

There is now no doubt in their minds. Jesus has made every effort to help these three to know that He is indeed the Son of God. After these soul-stirring events in the upper room, there can be no doubt: Jesus is Lord, the only son of the Father, the long-awaited Messiah.

When the disciples sing their final hymn and leave for their prayer vigil during the night of dark Gethsemane, James, Peter, and John are at the side of the Master. They always seem to be closest to their Lord. They always seem ready to go just a little farther than the others—these three: Peter and James and John.

Perhaps that is why Leonardo has placed James, the brother of John, here next to Jesus, to His left. "Sons of thunder," Jesus called these brothers. And you can see why. Here in this picture James is exploding in a double gesture of horror. He flings out his arms impulsively and asks the Master: "Is it I, Lord?"

Yet, of these three, James is usually the silent partner. Peter—the born leader. John—a man of warmth and depth, sure to make an impression. But James is a stalwart man of silence.

Though he says little, he is always there when he is needed most. How much we need these quiet men who make their witness by what they do more than by what they say!

James is such a man. James—the stalwart, the silent! Now he is stirred to action and speech by the announcement about the betrayer. He is saying: "Is it I, Lord?"

THOMAS

Thomas

Immediately behind James is Thomas, often called doubting Thomas. He stands at his place at the table and thrusts his way forward. He is waving a questioning finger in the face of Jesus as though to ask: "Lord, where are you going?" The inquisitive nature of this doubting disciple is magnificently interpreted by Leonardo da Vinci.

The truth is, the Bible tells us very little about Thomas until he comes to the upper room. He cannot believe the truth of the Master's words even on the night of the Last Supper.

He hears his Lord saying, "Little children, yet a little while I am with you." As his Master is speaking, we see the tortured look on Thomas' face, reflecting the struggle within his soul as he seeks to understand more of what Jesus is saying. Before he can speak, another disciple, Peter, asks his question for him: "Lord, where are you going?"

Jesus answers: "I am going where you cannot follow me just now, but you will later follow me."

Now Thomas is more confused; so Jesus says to the group: "Stop letting your hearts be troubled; keep on believing in God, and also in me. In my Father's house there are many dwelling places; if there were not, I would have told you. . . . I will come back and take you to be face to face with me, so that you may always be right where I am. And you know the way to the place where I am going" (Williams).

But Thomas blurts out his doubts, saying, "Lord, we do not know where you are going; how can we know the way?"

Jesus assures him, "I am the way, and the truth, and the life; no one comes to the Father, but by me. If you had known me, you would know my Father also; henceforth you know him and have seen him."

Later the crucifixion crushed Thomas. When he hears others tell of Jesus' resurrection, Thomas has his doubts. This good news is too good to be true. Thomas is not there when the Master appears on the first day of the week.

The disciples keep saying to Thomas, "We have seen the Lord!" But Thomas answered, "Unless I see the nailprints in His hands, and put my finger into them, and put my hand into His side, I will never believe it!" (Williams)

Just a week later the disciples were together in Jerusalem. Now Thomas was with them. Although the doors were bolted, Jesus appeared and stood among them. He speaks to Thomas, "Put your finger here . . . ; do not be faithless, but believing."

It is enough for Thomas. He sees "the light of the knowledge of the glory of God in the face of Christ." He makes no move to touch Jesus' wounds. Instead he makes his great affirmation of faith: "My Lord and my God!"

There is something of Thomas in all of us. How can we be sure of eternal life? How can we know the Father?

We find the answer to life's ultimate meaning as we see Jesus, who is saying to us—and to all doubting Thomases: "Blessed are those who have not seen, and yet believe."

PHILIP

Philip

Let us look again at the Master with His disciples at this their last meal together. Philip, too, has risen to his feet. He breaks into the conversation between Thomas and his Lord. Philip cannot understand this relationship between Jesus and the Father. What is this strange thing Jesus is saying: "If you had known me, you would have known my Father also." This is too much for Philip. "Lord, show us the Father."

The Philip we meet in the gospel story is a steady, hard-working, matter-of-fact type of person. He seems to be just a little slow to catch on to a big idea.

We meet Philip on the occasion of the feeding of the five thousand (John 6:1-13). This love feast, feeding of the five thousand, is a preview of the last-supper celebration just before Passover. Jesus lifts up His eyes and sees the multitude coming to Him. Seeking to test Philip, Jesus asks "How are we to buy bread, so that these people may eat?"

Philip answers, "Two hundred denarii [about forty dollars] would not buy enough bread for each of them to get a little."

Philip is the slow, plodding disciple. Even on the night of the Lord's Supper, he insists on a demonstration. A Father's house with many rooms? The Lord going to prepare a place for us? The Lord coming again to take us to Himself? How can we know the way? Jesus the way and the truth and the life? No one comes to the Father, but by the Son? If we know the Son, we have met His Father also? How can all these things be? These questions are whirling around in the mind of Philip. He must have some practical answer. He blurts out: "Lord, show us the Father, and we shall be satisfied."

How can Jesus possibly meet the question of Philip, who so often seems so slow of understanding, so tiresome in his tediousness? Philip wants a formula, something concrete and practical. What can Jesus say to show him who He is?

Now we see the anxious, inquiring face of Philip as he ponders Jesus' words. Leonardo's portraiture of Philip emphasizes the bewilderment in the gestures and face of the man. The Master talks as if He were going to be separated from them. Surely this cannot be. Philip's face shows how puzzled and confused he is.

Jesus remembers Philip's finest hour. It was just a few days ago. The Greeks had come to worship at the feast. Some of them came boldly up to Philip and said: "Sir, we wish to see Jesus." Immediately Philip told Andrew, and Andrew went with him and brought them to Jesus. Philip could think of no better answer to their question than to introduce them to the Son of Man face to face.

Now Philip himself is asking, "Lord, show us the Father."

Can this be the same Philip who met Nathanael's critical query "Can anything good come out of Nazareth?" with the answer, "Come and see"? He is saying now, "Lord, show us the Father, and we shall be satisfied."

Suddenly Jesus sees how He can answer Philip's puzzling doubts and take the dimness of his soul away. He will draw Philip a picture! Jesus paints this picture:

"Have I been with you so long, and yet you do not know me, Philip? He who has seen me has seen the Father; how can you say, 'Show us the Father'? Do you not believe that I am in the Father and the Father in me? The words that I say to you I do not speak on my own authority; but the Father who dwells in me does his works. Believe me that I am in the Father and the Father in me; or else believe me for the sake of the works themselves."

All of us, like Philip, want to know what God is like. Or like the Greeks at the Passover, "We wish to see Jesus."

Philip is saying to us, "Come and see."

Our Lord is saying to us: "He who has seen me has seen the Father." He is saying to us, as He said the day He first sought out Philip, "Follow me."

We who want to know what God is like can feast our eyes on Jesus. God put into the portrait of His Son all that the human frame can contain. Christ is God's best self-portrait.

We see James the silent, Thomas the doubter, and Philip the plodder form a physical and psychological entity at the table.

ANDREW, JAMES THE LESS, AND BARTHOLOMEW

Now our eyes move back across the table, past the irresistible features of the Master to the group at the far end of the table, to the Master's right. Here we meet, first, Andrew the usher; then, behind him, James the Less; and at the end of the table, standing up, Bartholomew the skeptic.

The farther you move from the Master at the center, the more obscure the disciples become. This group of three has two men who are little more than names in the Gospel accounts. We are not even sure of the name of the apostle represented by the figure at the end.

ANDREW

Andrew

Andrew was the first to exclaim: "We have found the Messiah." He sits at the end of the group beside James the Less. Andrew would be comparatively unknown, too, but for a paradoxical reason. He is a brother of a famous man. Every time we meet him he is introduced as Andrew, Simon Peter's brother. He is overshadowed by the stature of his famous brother; yet in his own quiet way Andrew is a significant person. As we study his record, we see that Andrew is, in fact, a disciple of distinction. His record found in the New Testament stands out for three noteworthy accomplishments.

When first we meet Andrew, he is introduced to Jesus by John the Baptist. Immediately, Andrew catches fire with enthusiasm for the Master. This Jesus lights for Andrew a whole new way of life. This new life is so filled with promise and purpose that he seeks out his brother Peter, according to the account given in the Gospel of John. Andrew knows that if Peter sees Jesus he, too, will love and follow Him.

BARTHOLOMEW, JAMES THE LESS, ANDREW

Andrew heard John say of Jesus: "Behold, the Lamb of God!" At this time Andrew was a devoted follower of John the Baptist; but when he heard this, he turned and followed Jesus. Jesus saw Andrew and the other disciples following Him, and said, "What do you seek?"

Andrew answered, "Rabbi, where are you staying?"

Jesus said, "Come and see." Andrew does just that. He spends the day with Jesus. What he sees and hears is so challenging that he immediately becomes a disciple of Jesus.

But that was not enough for Andrew. He finds his brother and brings him to Jesus. The first one Andrew introduced to Jesus was his own brother Simon. When Jesus saw Simon, He immediately gave him a new name. "So you are Simon the son of John?" He said. "You shall be called Cephas."

When next we meet Andrew, the usher in the Gospels, he is among the disciples and the crowds who are milling about the seashore where Jesus is preaching. They are wondering how they are going to have anything to eat. The disciples argue about what to do. It is Andrew who finds a lad and comes to the Master saying, "There is a lad here who has five barley loaves and two fish."

Jesus takes the boy's love gift of five loaves and two fish. He blesses them and gives the gift back—a thousandfold. Through the miracle of the breaking of bread and the gift of a little boy, the multitude is fed.

Bible scholars believe the feeding of the five thousand is a preview of things to come in the upper room. Thus, this sacrament of the Lord's Supper is not simply a mystical union of bread and wine, but a practical recognition of man's need: "Give us this day our daily bread."

Doubtless Andrew's mind is rushing back to that day when the Master first became known to him in the breaking of bread. This act takes on new meaning for Andrew as he sits here and sees the Master on this night of His betrayal take bread, bless it, break it, and give it to them, saying: "This is my body which is for you. Do this in remembrance of me."

Finally, the only glimpse we have of Andrew during the last week of Jesus' life is, as we have seen, when Philip comes to him with the word that there are "outsiders" wanting to come in. Characteristically, Andrew does not hesitate. He pins his usher's carnation on his lapel and goes at once to Jesus. He tells Him that there are people waiting with the request, "We wish to see Jesus." Andrew had the honor of being the first to invite other men to come to Jesus.

Today many churches have St. Andrew Clubs, or Fishermen's Clubs. Here small groups of Christians band themselves together in prayer and fellowship. Like Andrew, they also go out as evangelists, looking for those who are in need of Christ. What a splendid line these evangelists make—a line that reaches from the upper room to our own altar!

James the Less

JAMES THE LESS

James, the son of Alphaeus, or James the Less as we know him, is pictured behind Andrew. James reaches out his hand toward Simon Peter to get his attention. We know very little about this son of Alphaeus except that his mother was at the cross. He is not a speaker or actor in the passion drama. He is one of the relatively unknown among the apostles.

Even the name tradition has affixed to him—"the Less"—is obscure. Probably he got his name to keep him from being confused with the other disciple James, the son of Zebedee. It may be that this James was physically a small fellow. But our Lord looks not upon the outward appearance, but into the heart. What Jesus saw in James was so fine that he called him "Friend" and invited him to become a disciple in "The Beloved Society."

One of the most difficult things to do is to overcome some physical handicap. Some groups in our world measure a man by his height and weight. With them size counts. But the Christian measure of a man does not count weight and height. You cannot put love on the scales! Try measuring mathematically how much parents love their children.

Some of the world's greatest men have been small in stature. Take Napoleon at one extreme or John Wesley at the other— the man who exploited the French Revolution and the man who kept England from a similar revolution. Small in stature! Great in influence!

Much that we know about James the Less is legendary. Many have made the assumption that James the Less or James the son of Alphaeus and James the brother of Jesus were the same person. With this assumption, they have identified the martyrdom and symbols of James the brother of Jesus with James the Less.

The early historian Hegesippus says the executioners of James the brother of Jesus got him on top of the Temple and pushed him off. He was injured but staggered to his feet. His enemies then stoned him, with someone giving him the fatal blow with a fuller's bat. To this account tradition has added that the body was sawn asunder.

The New Testament record presents James the son of Alphaeus and James the brother of Jesus as two men—not the same person. Here is a disciple so unknown that the symbol most widely used to represent him—the saw—belongs to another man (see James the Less, page 61). Yet the life of James the Less, by his size and obscurity, represents many unknown thousands of Christians: persons known only to God, who have served worthily and have put their shoulders to the wheel in performance of duty, without praise or applause. The Lord needs such disciples. Thank God for the unknown soldiers in the Lord's company. That classification includes most of us!

Bartholomew

BARTHOLOMEW

Here we have another of the comparatively unknown at the Lord's table. Tradition names him as the thinker of the group. Actually he is little more than a name in the chosen company.

The three Synoptic Gospels—Matthew, Mark, Luke—and Acts call him Bartholomew. The Gospel of John does not so name him but tells about Jesus calling a man named Nathanael to be His follower. This leads many to believe that Bartholomew and Nathanael were the same person. Perhaps Bartholomew was the man's family name and Nathanael his given name. Though the Gospel of John is our only source for insights into the character of this man, we shall call him Bartholomew rather than Nathanael as John identifies him.

Regardless of what we call him, we meet here a man who has a mind set about religion. Leonardo shows him here after he had sprung to his feet, clutching the edge of the table and lurching forward. Now he stands stark still, stupified. He is trying to probe the suddenly raised and difficult problem that the Master has thrown out to them. A betrayer? Who? Why? How? Bartholomew wants to know. Yet he is speechless.

Bartholomew has not always been so interested in the Messiahship of Jesus. When he first heard about it, he could not believe his ears. Nazareth? Everyone laughed at the thought that anything good could come from such a town. Does not everyone know that Nazareth is just a little insignificant place that does not amount to anything? It is absurd to think that any good thing or any important person can come from there.

This was what Bartholomew thought—that is, until that moment when he met the Master face to face.

Bartholomew can never forget that day Philip found him and said, "We have found him of whom Moses in the law and also the prophets wrote, Jesus of Nazareth, the son of Joseph."

"Can anything good come out of Nazareth?" Bartholomew asked his friend.

Philip answered, "Come and see."

Jesus sees our friend approaching; He says of him, "Behold, an Israelite indeed, in whom there is no guile!"

This was a remarkable thing to say, was it not? Jesus did not say anything like this about any of the other disciples in the beginning. Bartholomew was astonished. He could not believe his ears. "How do you know me?"

Jesus replied, "Before Philip called you, when you were under the fig tree, I saw you."

"Rabbi, you are the Son of God! You are the King of Israel!"

The Master said, "Because I said to you, I saw you under the fig tree, do you believe? You shall see greater things than these."

That promise is being fulfilled before his eyes now in the upper room as Jesus takes the sacred cup and says, "Drink of it, all of you; for this is my blood of the new covenant, which is poured out for many for the forgiveness of sins."

Now Bartholomew knows what Jesus means when He says: "Truly, truly, I say to you, you will see heaven opened, and the angels of God ascending and descending upon the Son of man!" Jesus is actually affirming, beyond doubt, that He is the Son of God!

Matthew, Thaddaeus, Simon the Zealot

MATTHEW, THADDAEUS, AND SIMON THE ZEALOT

Far to the Master's left is a fourth group of disciples. They are trembling with excitement. Who can imagine this never-to-be-forgotten moment when Jesus takes the cup after supper, saying, "This cup is the new covenant in my blood. Do this, as often as you drink it, in remembrance of me."

While these four groups are separate and well-defined, they are all united in subtle ways. Every line of the picture converges on the face of Christ. The gestures of the apostles lead us back to Him. Matthew is boldly pointing in His direction. Thaddaeus jerks his thumb toward the center of the table. Simon the Zealot, at the end of the table, is facing his Lord. These make up the fourth and last group of disciples.

MATTHEW

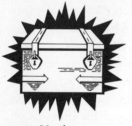

Matthew

Here is a man few people love. Citizens passing by his gate look on him with bitter grudging. Religious people watching him at work can only see him as a renegade servant of the government. The government looks upon him as a necessary evil. But one day a stranger comes who looks upon him as a man. Matthew feels a tap on his shoulder. He hears the sound of a voice, "Follow me." *
He sees a face, and straightway he rises. He is a new man from this day forward. This publican turned saint is chosen as one of the guests of honor invited to the upper room to break bread at the Last Supper with the Master of men.

Matthew's former job was a dirty, despised one. "Publican" is one of the most scorned words in the New Testament. Matthew's job was tax collecting until he found a more im-

---

* Here again, the names of the disciples are not consistent in the gospels. See Matthew 9:1-13 where the tax collector is called Matthew. See also parallels in Mark 2:13-17 and Luke 5:27-32 where Levi the son of Alphaeus and Levi are used as the names of one who is obviously the same man.

portant calling and a heartwarming fellowship beckoning him. That call "Follow me" was never clearer than on this night of the Lord's Supper.

With remorse Matthew remembers his old life. He was hated by his own people. Yet his job paid him well. He was on his way to a successful government career—at a time when his own countrymen were finding it hard to eke out a bare living, paying taxes as high as forty per cent of their wages. Matthew knew he was just at the threshold of financial security—and yet he was wretched. And then it happened!

"Follow me," the Master said. And Matthew got up and followed Him. Since that day when the Master's shadow first fell across his desk, Matthew was another man. Perhaps he even changed his name in honor of the event. The Gospels of Mark and Luke identify this tax collector turned disciple of Jesus as "Levi" or "Levi the son of Alphaeus." But the Gospel According to Matthew calls him Matthew.

But regardless of the explanation for the two names, this man comes to discover that this was the best bargain he ever made. He has exchanged his publican wretchedness for the dignity of discipleship. He has exchanged his business of collecting tax money for the exciting vocation of changing sinners into saints. He has deserted dishonesty and found the way and the truth and the life. He has left his life as a publican to do the work of an evangelist. This is the best bargain of his life. He tells others of this newfound life.

The experience of peace and joy that he found in his new vocation overflowed into the Gospel that bears his name. The Gospel According to Matthew stands first in the New Testament. Early in the second century Matthew's name was attached to this Gospel. Some of the work of the Apostle Matthew may have been included in this Gospel. Many scholars are of the opinion that Matthew did not give us the Gospel in its present form. The Gospel of Matthew forms a bridge between the Old Testament and the New Testament—of the New Covenant, as it might be translated. The First Gospel bears the imprint of the personality of this great evangelist. Its author seeks to affirm that Jesus is the long-awaited Lawgiver-Teacher-King-Messiah.

Jesus is the great Lawgiver the Gospel is saying. This great book affirms the new law written on the inner life. The book is divided into five great portions to take the place of the five books of the Law—the *Pentateuch*.

Jesus is King. Royal blood flows in His veins. David is His ancestor.

Jesus is the Messiah. Matthew sees Jesus' mission clearly on this last night as he hears his Lord say: "The Son of man came not to be served but to serve, and to give his life as a ransom for many."

In this magnificent portrait of *The Last Supper*, we are looking into the face of the new Matthew. Here is a witness for Christ. This is not the first festive meal Matthew has attended. After his decision to follow Christ, he called for a celebration. He wasted no time in letting his old friends of the custom house know about this change in his life. He had a banquet for them. Matthew invited his old friends in and he introduced them to his new Master.

He knows what it means to an Israelite to sit down and break bread with a friend. This act is a sacred covenant, so sacred that it constitutes an unwritten law—the law of hospitality. Break bread with another man and you are pledged to him with your life, with bonds of love and loyalty.

This is why Matthew shows such astonishment. He seems to be whispering to Thaddaeus and Simon: "Did you hear what He is saying? One of us has broken the sacred covenant! One of us has betrayed Him unto death!"

THADDAEUS

Thaddaeus

Another of those personalities among Jesus' followers of whom we know little is Thaddaeus. He moves in the shadows at the edge of the group. Judas Thaddaeus, they call him.

But here he is at the table of the Lord. He is among the twelve who break bread with Jesus at the Last Supper. Something the Master says arouses him to speak out. He wants to know why Jesus is revealing Himself just to this inner group of disciples instead of to the whole world.

Thaddaeus had been greatly impressed by the public ovation that began outside Bethany and burst into a triumphal entry into the Holy City. This was Sunday, just a few days ago. Thaddaeus and the others were so sure then that Jesus' hour had fully come. They thought this turn of events would climax with Jesus ascending to the throne of David and becoming King of Israel.

But now the Master is talking of something entirely different from what they have imagined and dreamed. Jesus goes so far as to say: "Little children, yet a little while I am with you." He tells them as He has told the Jews, "Where I am going you cannot come."

But Judas Thaddaeus is shocked when he hears Jesus say: "Yet a little while, and the world will see me no more, but you will see me; because I live, you will live also."

Thaddaeus can stand the suspense no longer. He blurts out his question, breaking into the last-supper discourse, "Lord, how is it that you will manifest yourself to us, and not to the world?"

Jesus answers him: "If a man loves me, he will keep my word, and my Father will love him, and we will come to him and make our home with him. He who does not love me does not keep my words; and the word which you hear is not mine but the Father's who sent me."

This one view we have of Thaddaeus at the table stands out in bold relief. His question is answered. Jesus goes on to say: "These things I have spoken to you, while I am still with you. But the Counselor, the Holy Spirit, whom the Father will send in my name, he will teach you all things, and bring to your remembrance all that I have said to you."

Little does Thaddaeus realize how this promise of Jesus is to be fulfilled in an upper room when the day of Pentecost fully comes a little more than fifty days after this farewell meal.

Thaddaeus and the others will remember forever Jesus' final word to them in the upper room discourse:

"But when the Counselor comes, whom I shall send to you from the Father, . . . he will bear witness to me; and you also are witnesses, because you have been with me from the beginning."

Simon the Zealot

SIMON THE ZEALOT

One of the last men we would expect to find in the upper room is Simon the Zealot. He is the last man at the end of the table. Simon the Zealot's name betrays the fact that he has belonged to the patriotic party that fears and hates Rome. His name Zealot tells us that he is one of these fanatic patriots who believes that the Kingdom of Israel and the Kingdom of God are the same.

Yet Jesus chose Simon the Zealot, and we find his name recorded in all the lists of the twelve. Jesus enrolled him in a school for Christian living. He took him into that fellowship someone calls "The Beloved Society." There Simon begins to see that those who take the sword perish with the sword. Jesus' problem with Simon is the number one problem our Lord has with His world: It seems easier and surer to trust in the way of hate than it does to trust the way of love. Yet the testimony for peace in the New Testament is one of the most eloquent witnesses the Bible makes.

Get the picture as Simon sees it: for a thousand years the people of Israel have longed to be free. God chose them as His people. They chose *Yahweh,* God. They made a covenant. God promised His people that He would deliver them, redeem them, give them their freedom, and give back to them the Promised Land. To a loyal Israelite that means throwing out the Romans, setting up a kingdom as the Maccabean tried to do, and pushing back the boundaries of their beloved land to the place in the sun Israel held under their great King David. The way to do this, obviously, is by force. That is the only language the Romans understand—revolution. Get our guns and join the army. How modern this all sounds!

"The kingdom come!" This was a battle cry for the Zealots; but Jesus did everything He could to discourage this kind of following, this kind of movement.

In His greatest sermon He says, "Blessed are the peacemakers, for they shall be called sons of God." "You have heard that it was said, 'An eye for an eye and a tooth for a tooth.' But I say to you, Do not resist one who is evil. But if any one strikes you on the right cheek, turn to him the other also." "You have heard that it was said, 'You shall love your neighbor and hate your enemy.' But I say to you, Love your enemies and pray for those who persecute you, so that you may be sons of your Father who is in heaven."

Jesus was careful to ask the disciples and those who were healed to say nothing in public about His unique mission as

Messiah. He did not want to be identified with the false nationalistic messiahs who sprung up on every hand. He said to the healed leper: "See that you say nothing to any one."

Somewhere along the way Simon the Zealot began to discover Jesus was not working for the kind of kingdom he hoped for. Perhaps it was on the road to Jerusalem that Simon finally saw his hopes dashed to earth. Jesus made it clear that He was not going to take the city by force. He spent His final hours hammering into the heads of the disciples the kind of Son of Man He is to be, "Mocked and scourged and crucified." "The Son of man came not to be served but to serve, and to give his life a ransom for many."

The people of Israel hold so many ideas of what the role of the Messiah should be. But for Simon some of the roles of the Messiah were ruled out by all the things the Master had been teaching. The covenant Jesus makes with His disciples reveals to Simon the role the Master is choosing to play. Jesus deliberately chooses to take the full consequences for being the suffering servant!

The high priestly prayer of Jesus, recorded in the seventeenth chapter of the Gospel According to John, takes on a new and glorious light in this setting. As Jesus closes His prayer, He says:

"O righteous Father, the world has not known thee, but I have known thee; and these know that thou hast sent me. I made known to them thy name, and I will make it known, that the love with which thou hast loved me may be in them, and I in them."

JESUS CHRIST

IV

JESUS CHRIST

Our eyes are drawn back to the Master, though they have not been far from Him in any of our considerations. In the midst of our study of the life of Leonardo, this masterpiece of his, and the twelve apostles, we have met the towering presence of the Master. We have studied the life of Leonardo because of his incomparable portraiture of the Last Supper. We have looked at each of the apostles in the presence of Christ.

We have felt Christ's transforming presence at work as we have seen Him reach out and touch the lives of these men. Here is God with us, God making a personal appearance through His Son.

We have seen how Leonardo placed Christ at the center of the picture. He put the Master in front of the large window so that He is flooded with light. All the lines of the picture converge on Him. Christ's shocking statement to them, "One of you will betray me," motivates each group's conversation and action.

Now look more closely at Leonardo's picture of the Master of men. We are deeply moved by Leonardo's face of the Savior, sometimes called the saddest face in all history. He seems sad, submissive, forgiving, as though He is hopeful that even yet Judas may repent in his heart before it is too late. Our hearts approve this touch Leonardo's brush gives to the face of Jesus. We know that He who later prayed, "Father, forgive them; for they know not what they do," for those who were crucifying Him would do no less for Judas who was preparing to deliver Him up to be crucified.

The head of Christ was the despair of Leonardo. He struggled mightily with his interpretation of Jesus' face and features. He searched for the radiant features of Christ among the aristocratic youth of Milan. There is a tradition that Leonardo expressed his despair at not being able to find someone with the radiant features of Christ to his friend Zenale. The tradition says Zenale advised him: "The mistake you have made, Leonardo, is so great that only God can repair it. It is not in your power or that of anyone else to represent a higher measure of beauty and divinity than you have already given James the Greater and James the Less. Therefore, you ought to let well enough alone and leave the Christ incomplete."

> Vainly my pencil struggles to express
> The sorrowing grandeur of such holiness.
> In patient thought, in every seeking prayer
> I strive to shape that glorious face within;
> But the soul's mirror dulled and dimmed by sin
> Reflects not yet the perfect image there.

Leonardo left his painting of Christ incomplete. He did not feel worthy to paint such wonderful things as the eyes of Christ; so they are downcast. His original design shows a beardless Christ with a warm, youthful face, frank and open. The saddest yet most sensitive face in all of art is pictured here.

Leonardo searched for hands to use as models for painting the hands of Christ, and he records in his notebook about finding them. Christ's right hand, palm downward, seems to say, "If it be possible, let this cup pass from me." His left hand, upturned, seems to suggest, "Nevertheless, not as I will, but as thou wilt." Christ's hands alone tell the story of the human and divine natures that meet in Him.

We are confronted with a mystery. We cannot fully understand how God could become man in Jesus Christ. But when we see Christ, we know that the fullness of God dwells in

Him. This is the miracle God wants to perform in each of us. The purpose of the incarnation is that we may be in Christ. We partake of the sacrament of His body and blood in remembrance of Him. When we come to Christ's table to commune, we come with a prayer that we may be filled with the fullness of His life, may grow into His likeness, and may evermore dwell in Him and He in us.

We can understand why the author of First John breaks into a hymn of praise and thanksgiving: "Beloved, we are God's children now; it does not yet appear what we shall be, but we know that when he appears we shall be like him, for we shall see him as he is."

V

THE STORY OF THE HANDS
IN THE PICTURE

Notice how skillfully the artist expresses the emotions of the men by their hands. Their hands alone tell the story. Having already looked at the hands of Jesus, let us read the story the hands of the disciples tell.

John has his hands folded upon the table in submissive innocence. Judas clutches the moneybag with his right hand. In the original painting, Judas overturns the saltcellar with his elbow. Peter impulsively reaches for John with his left hand and holds in the other hand his knife with its handle against Judas' back.

James the Greater flings his hands out in a double gesture of surprise. Thomas thrusts an inquiring finger into the face of Jesus, demanding, "Lord, where are you going?" Philip's hands, pointing to himself, seem to emphasize his burning question: "Lord, show us the father, and we shall be satisfied."

Andrew's hands, said to be among the most handsome in all art, are outstretched before him in an expression of disdain. James the Less is stretching out his hand behind Andrew to Peter. Bartholomew is clutching the table to steady himself with his hands.

Matthew points with both hands to the Savior in an effort to emphasize what he is saying. Thaddaeus is pointing his thumb toward Jesus. Simon the Zealot, who has reason to be puzzled by this strange turn of events, lifts his hands in a helpless gesture of resignation.

VI

HOW DID THEY DIE?

Call the roll!

What happened to these twelve? How did they die? We have already looked at Judas and his betrayal of the Master. In Matthew 27:5, we are told that Judas hanged himself. What was the fate of these other men who went everywhere to tell men how the Master lived, died, and was raised from the dead?

Let us call the roll as we see them march by in an endless line of splendor. With the exception of James the brother of John, we have only what tradition says as to how these apostles died.

First, there is Simon, called also Peter. Tradition says he was crucified on an upside-down cross in Rome.

Andrew, Peter's brother—crucified on an X-shaped cross.

James the Greater—put to death by Herod with a sword.

John—probably the only apostle to die a natural death.

Philip—a martyr tradition says, but it does not agree as to how he died. One tradition says he was crucified, another says he died by the spear.

Bartholomew—beaten to death in Armenia.

Matthew—crucified on a Tau cross in Ethiopia.

Thomas—run through with a lance in India.

James the Less—his death is as much a mystery as his identity. One tradition has him martyred in Egypt. Another confuses him with James the brother of Jesus, and has him beaten to death and sawn asunder.

Simon the Zealot—sawn asunder or beheaded.

Thaddaeus—martyred with a lance or a halberd.

THE UPPER ROOM CHAPEL WOOD CARVING OF *TH*

ast Supper, REPRODUCED BY HOWARD W. ELLIS

These are the men the Master invited to be with Him at the last-supper table. If we had had no knowledge of their lives after Jesus was raised from the grave, who of us would have expected them to come through like this? Not a bad record, is it, for these men who when Jesus was seized by the authorities forsook Him and fled?

Even Matthias, elected by the disciples to take Judas' place, after Judas took his own life, is said to have been stoned. Paul, Apostle to the Gentiles, made his final journey to Rome where he was imprisoned and put to death by the Roman authorities.

VII

SHIELDS FOR THE TWELVE

The apostles' shields, too, tell the story of the life and death of each apostle. The shields used here are pictures of the apostles' shields on the chancel rail in The Upper Room Chapel. In the place of the shield of Judas, the chancel rail carries the shield of Paul, Apostle to the Gentiles.

PETER

Peter has his upside-down cross, reminding us of his request to be crucified this way because he did not feel worthy to die in the same position as his Lord. The crossed keys are for Peter's confession at Caesarea Phillipi.

ANDREW

Tradition says *Andrew* was crucified on an X-shaped cross; therefore this type cross is called Andrew's Cross.

JAMES THE GREATER

Three scallop shells on the shield of *James the Greater* represent his pilgrimages and his missionary journeys.

JOHN

John's shield holds the chalice and serpent, recalling the legend about him. He was sentenced to die by poisoning, but he made the sign of the cross, and the poison escaped in the form of a serpent.

PHILIP

Philip is usually represented by a cross and two loaves of bread, commemorating the feeding of the five thousand and Philip's part in it. Philip's shield in The Upper Room Chapel has two shocks of wheat on it instead of the two loaves.

THOMAS

Thomas has his carpenter's square and a spear, representing his building activities for the Church and the mode of his death.

BARTHOLOMEW

Bartholomew has his book—an open Bible—and a flaying knife. The Bible tells us of his faith in God's Word, and the flaying knife was the instrument used in his martyrdom.

MATTHEW

Matthew is symbolized by three purses, a reminder of his occupation as tax collector before he answered the Master's call, "Follow me."

JAMES THE LESS

The saw is the symbol for *James the Less*. However, recent research indicates that James the Less has been confused with James the brother of Jesus who was beaten to death with a fuller's bat and then sawn asunder. James the Less himself probably was killed in Egypt.

SIMON THE ZEALOT

Simon the Zealot's shield shows a fish lying on a book. The book signifies the gospel and the fish that he was a fisher of men for the Master.

THADDAEUS

Thaddaeus, sometimes called Jude, is represented by a sailing vessel, representing his missionary journeys.

PAUL

Paul's shield contains a rayed cross, representing his spreading the gospel through his preaching and missionary journeys.

We stated at the first of the chapter that the chancel rail carries Paul's shield instead of that of Judas.

Judas' shield shows his disgrace. One often used for him bears his moneybag with his despised thirty pieces of silver, the reminder of his betrayal of Jesus.

Here, then, are the twelve men the Master chose to be with Him and to go out with His message; and with them is the Apostle Paul whom He chose to take His message of salvation to the Gentiles. Here are members—leaders—of the first Christian Church.

Matthew groups them in pairs in connection with the first mission Jesus sent them on:

First, Simon, who is called Peter, and Andrew his brother;
James the son of Zebedee, and John his brother;
Philip and Bartholomew;
Thomas and Matthew the tax collector;
James the son of Alphaeus, and Thaddaeus;
Simon the Cananaean, and Judas Iscariot, who betrayed him.

Though it was a dark moment both for Jesus and for His apostles when the Master said to them, "One of you will betray me," all was not dark. Being with Jesus made an amazing difference with eleven of the twelve. T. R. Glover, in *The Jesus of History*, speaks for us on this matter: "The greatest miracle in history seems to me the transformation that Jesus effected in those men. Everything else in Christian or secular history, compared to it, seems easy and explicable; and it was achieved by the love of Jesus."

Leonardo da Vinci made vivid as only a master could the moment during the Last Supper when Jesus said to His disciples, "One of you will betray me."

It was in the upper room that the tragedy and triumph of the gospel came to focus. It was in this room at the Last Supper that the disciples heard the Master make the shocking statement that one of them would betray Him. It was perhaps the place in Jerusalem where the disciples met their risen Lord, "Jesus himself stood among them" (Luke 24:36). Tradition tells us that this was the upper room in which the disciples were gathered on the day of Pentecost when they were made aware of the presence of the Holy Spirit.

When we see Christ's hands and look into His face, we come to understand why the Christian community comes to know Him in the breaking of bread and the taking of the cup.